FROM SHY

TO HI

TAME SOCIAL ANXIETY, MEET NEW PEOPLE AND BUILD SELF-CONFIDENCE

BY MICHAL STAWICKI

www.expandbeyondyourself.com

August 2014
Copyright © 2014 Michal Stawicki
All rights reserved worldwide.
ISBN: 1507825501
ISBN-13: 978-1507825501

Table of Contents

4

Introduction

Why This Book Exists

Shyness is a widespread problem. Our modern lifestyle fosters shyness over interaction. We are increasingly surrounded by machines and immersed in the online, impersonal world. For anyone living under the dark spell of shyness, it's a deep issue.

Shyness originates in the psyche, and though the pharmaceutical companies would like for you to believe that you can just pop a pill and banish your timidness, true change must come from within. Perhaps you have tried these pharmaceutical 'band-aids,' or perhaps, like most who suffer from shyness, you don't even consider it fixable. It's just part of your nature, right? "I was just created that way," you say.

But shyness is curable. You were not born that way. Somewhere along the way, you nurtured shyness within yourself, possibly without knowing. Perhaps others labeled you as shy and you bought into that assessment. However it came about, you do have the power to reverse your timidness and find confidence in your dealings with others.

The shyness affliction comes in many shades, but if you are the type of loner who feels awkward while interacting with new people, and who avoids unknown social situations at all costs, then this book will help you – if you choose to allow it. Anxiety may be a part of your internal constitution right now, but people change. You can change, too. What is more, you can design your change. You can choose how far you take the process, and progress at a pace that is comfortable for you. You don't need to become a total badass overnight.

This book is designed to help you, a shy person, develop the regular practice of meeting and talking to strangers. People who are already confident in new social situations do not need my advice; they already know the benefits of this confidence. By practicing this discipline, you, too, will come to know the benefits as you expand your circle of interaction and influence.

First of all, talking to strangers will impact your internal world. Our actions determine our state of mind and our attitudes. Currently, part of your definition of yourself is, "I'm a shy person." Imagine how your life will change when you see an internal shift to, "I'm confident while dealing with other people."

Tiny changes in your behavior, in your interactions and relationships, will fuel big change. *"Dripping water hollows out stone, not through force but through persistence."* The same goes with changing your attitude. Grandiose actions are not required. You do not need to give a speech to the masses tomorrow; you only need consistency.

The change in you will inspire changes in others. It's unavoidable. We are all connected. Your success and example will change others. Your success will lead you to new people and influence them. The lives of people you don't even know yet will be touched. Your influence will spread like ripples on a pond. I have seen it firsthand, and you will, too.

This change is enough to shake the world, and we don't have to start a political movement to drive this change. Collective change in many individuals is a powerful force, but collective change in many always springs from internal change in one. Recall John Lennon's song, "Imagine."

> "Imagine all the people,
> sharing all the world ...
> You may say I'm a dreamer,
> but I'm not the only one.
> I hope some day you'll join us,
> and the world will live as one."

That's the influence of one individual at work. It starts from a single person and spreads through society, changing the hearts of individuals one by one. All that's needed to realize John's vision is a change in a single human, and then the next and the next and the next, until "all the people" share similar values.

I don't preach any philosophy or religion. It's all about your personal impact on global society, an impact that is held back only by your clinging to shyness.

The influence and interaction game is an inside-out kind of thing. You can't impose on others what or how to think. But, you can share your opinion – not just with your words – but also (more importantly) through your deeds. That's how it works. People admired by society at large – Saint Teresa of Calcutta, Gandhi, Nelson Mandela, Martin Luther King Jr., Stephen R. Covey, to name a few – acted on that principle. They all were great influencers; people who left indelible marks on the progress of human society.

There are others who have different opinions. They prefer to manipulate, browbeat and deceive in order to influence people. They try to convince the world that their approach is quicker, easier and more effective. Many prominent politicians fall into this category.

At the core of every upheaval, there is a person who started it. Just one person. The world needs YOU, your unique voice and your interaction with other people, so you can influence your community, your country, our world.

This book is about gaining confidence by overcoming your shyness. It means building your mindset and attitudes through internal change, not by mastering tricks of manipulation. Manipulation and deceit will be unveiled in time; a change of mindset will serve you for a lifetime and have effects that ripple through our world long after you are gone.

You will find here my journey and my advice, but you are not obliged to conform to it. Your job is to pick up what will work for **you**, in your unique circumstances, and begin your own journey to self confidence.

Confessions of a Shy Guy

I used to be quite shy. As an introvert, I've always been inclined to refer to my internal world first and refer to other people much later (if ever). It's not that I'm heartless; when I finally recognized others around me, I found I cared deeply for them. I realized I could relate to them. My heart sunk each time I saw people less fortunate than me. But, because of my conditioning, the times when I truly saw them were rare. And, when I did really see them, I found myself lacking the social skills to begin an interaction.

One vivid example says it all. Several years ago, I was heading home from work – a 30- mile commute. That day, I missed my train and had to wait almost an hour for the next one. On the same platform, probably waiting for the same train, were a young lady and her sick son. The boy was maybe three years old, about the same age as my own sons.

His bald head and frightfully thin frame told me he likely had cancer. Even the effort of raising a bottle of Coke to his lips caused his hand to tremble. He paused drinking to vomit in a plastic bag.

This young child was suffering like I have never suffered in my life. His mother was caring, but firm. She held his head tightly when he vomited to avoid a resulting mess.

My heart dropped. I pitied them so much – mother and child both suffering so greatly there on that platform. I wanted deeply to talk to his mother, to offer her an encouraging word or a friendly chat to distract her temporarily. I wanted to tell the boy that I had two sons his age and that I thought they could become good friends ... but I couldn't. My own shyness prevented me from lifting another's spirits. I was unable to approach people I didn't know; unable to embrace the vulnerability required to reach out.

I actively talked myself out of trying to offer what I could to them: "If you walked up to them, what would you say? That you are sorry for them? Words are cheap. And what have you to offer? Money? You are not rich. Time? You are a 9 to 5 slave. Encouragement? Can you cure the boy?"

I didn't speak to them that day; didn't express my compassion for them. If that had happened today, it would be a different story.

So, what changed? I changed.

Was it difficult? Yes, a bit. Was the change worthwhile? Absolutely.

Why do I tell you this story? Because we both know that being shy sucks, and this story, to me, best illustrates that. It's not my only example by any means, and they all left me with a sour taste in my mouth. I consider myself a Christian. I often felt my faith dictated that I try to offer comfort to others in hardship. For that reason, it stung even worse when I was unable to. I would like to say that this event shook me so hard that I was transformed from that moment on. It would have fit the stereotypes we worship – instant gratification, an easy fix.

In truth, I lived with my shyness several more years. I preferred hiding in my own world over reaching out to other people. It was uncomfortable. Human relationships were always a little puzzling to me. Social rituals always tired me. Diplomacy is not my strong suit. I usually say what I have on my mind. Often, it's not the thing people want to hear. I retreated to my internal world; it's my natural environment. I kept interaction limited to my closest family, a handful of friends, my brothers and sisters in my church community, and colleagues. I functioned that way for years.

I thought I could operate in that mode for the rest of my life. After all, I had my basic social needs satisfied. I didn't need strangers in my life; was indifferent to their existence. I recognized them only when I needed something from them: the shopkeeper in the grocery store, the guy on the full train occupying two seats, new colleagues in a new job – this was the limit of my social interactions.

Whether it was indifference or laziness is hard to say. I was relatively happy being in my small circle of relationships and my own mind. I associated every attempt to meet new people with unneeded effort, struggle and nuisance.

Shyness very often feels cozy. It allows you to shelter yourself in your own world without interacting with any of those 'odd' people around you. When you retreat, nobody can hurt you, right? But shyness is far from a blessing. Quite the opposite – in the long run, it's a self-imposed curse.

It's as true for you as it was for me. You don't need strangers in your life; you can live without them. But, allowing others into your life is required for growth. You grow only by embracing change, and there is no more unpredictable factor on this planet than another human being with his own free will, his own mind, his imagination and unique story.

In short – interaction with others is enriching.

Shyness is just one part of your internal construction, but you can rebuild yourself and overcome it. I know, because I transformed my own life. While still introverted, I consider myself outgoing rather than a retreating turtle. I still prefer my own company, but I'm no longer allergic to people I don't know.

A word of caution here – I'm not a 'regular' shy guy. I'm quite comfortable with public speaking, the biggest fear for most people. Training a group of new people at work or presenting to a class has never intimidated me very much.

I studied in two different cities, then moved twice for my career. In each of those cities, I was a member of a different church community. These communities relied quite heavily on speaking before the group. I was perfectly comfortable with that, partially because I immediately accepted them into my inner circle as my brothers in Christ, but also because I'm not generally afraid of public speaking.

One-on-one personal interactions with new people, however? Terrifying.

There is Hope – My Transformation

When I decided to change my life, I decided also to confront the shyness that devoured any hope I had of connecting with others. In recognizing my renewed drive for growth, I saw how my shyness restricted me – an obstacle between me and the man I wanted to be. I also sensed that my behavior was flawed; it was against all my beliefs to be so reserved. I wanted to redeem myself. The memory of that trembling boy, weak and vomiting on the train platform was imprinted on my soul. My simultaneous desire and fear to reach out was an experience I didn't want to repeat ever again. Having deep reserves of compassion for the less-fortunate, but the inability to express them properly, wore on my heart.

When I set out to bring change to my life, I designed my daily disciplines around principles in Jeff Olson's, *The Slight Edge*. One of the six habits I challenged myself to from the very beginning was talking to strangers. I gritted my teeth, mobilized my willpower, and sought occasions to talk to new people every day.

I fell flat on my face.

I started too ambitiously for my timid, reserved personality. I was in no position to talk to strangers.

The thought of approaching someone and opening my mouth paralyzed me. Each time I tried, my heart beat faster; my hands shook and butterflies raced in my stomach. Even thinking about those early experiences now causes my body to tense. Perhaps you know these feelings?

Talking to a stranger seemed to be the toughest, most impossible act in the universe.

But, I had my newfound sense of purpose; I was determined. With that attitude, I was able to force myself to talk with strangers a few times. I felt stunned after every successful attempt, but also exhausted.

I approached this like the average New Year's resolution. You grit your teeth and do the unpleasant new activity. It's not fun at all, but you feel like you achieved something, because you forced yourself to do it and overcame your limitations... And then, you fail a couple of times and decide that it's not such a big deal. You allow yourself a cheat day, a cheat week and before you know it, you're back where you began. And perhaps, worse off – if you then consider yourself a failure and beat yourself up, you are likely to subconsciously avoid any future attempts. You might continue to do your new activity randomly, when you feel like it. You lie to yourself and say that next week ... next month ... next quarter, you will get serious about it.

I faced this problem myself, but confronted it by habit-tracking. I started to track my disciplines. I used just a sheet of paper with the list of my habits-in-construction, each day ticking them off when I succeeded, or writing a minus sign when I failed. I tasked myself with talking to strangers every day.

Going through my notes after a few weeks, I realized that I had a lot more minuses in the 'talk to strangers' category than in all other habits put together. There was something wrong with my approach in that discipline. I examined my attempts, my results, and decided I was not ready to talk to strangers yet. Attempting it was draining my energy and undermining my self-confidence rather than driving growth.

This caused great internal anxiety. On one hand, I was all about transforming my life. On the other, I was already stumbling, and this was the first change I was attempting.

Habit-tracking allowed me to realize all of this consciously, kept it in my awareness. Habit tracking prevents you from pushing the habit back into the subconscious, where it will be deeply hidden – your brain's attempt to avoid unpleasant outcomes.

I realized that I was simply unable to talk to strangers on a daily basis – I was too afraid of it. It just wasn't as easy (or enjoyable, at the time) as studying the Bible for 10 minutes a day (another discipline I started). I had to change my approach.

Having this mental feedback, I could redesign my discipline. I painstakingly planned it from scratch. I'm a firm believer in consistency and continuity, so it remained on my list of daily actions.

But this time I started small. Because talking to strangers was too ambitious for me, I committed to just making eye contact with a stranger and smiling at him or her. I was so socially awkward that even this was challenging. Better, but I still collected some minuses in my tracking sheet. I didn't want to stop at smiling, so I set three levels of difficulty. Level 1: The relatively passive activity of making eye contact and smiling. Level 2: Chip in on an existing conversation. Level 3: "The hard level:" Start a conversation with a stranger.

I gave a lot of time and attention to details like this to rejuvenate the discipline. This was the key. As Abraham Lincoln said: *"Give me six hours to chop down a tree and I will spend the first four sharpening the axe."*

Shyness and the Road to Confidence

Defining Shyness
Jim Rohn firmly believed that the etymology of a word says a lot about the concept it represents. The word "shy" derives from the Proto-Germanic *skeukh(w)az*, which means "afraid." Many languages followed suit: the late Old English *sceoh* – "timid, easily startled," the German *scheuchen* – "to scare away," the Old French *eschiver* – "to shun," and the Italian *schivare* – "to avoid."

Shyness is rooted in fear. Modern, psychological definitions confirm this:

"The primary defining characteristic of shyness is a largely ego-driven fear of what other people will think of a person's behavior, which results in the person becoming scared of doing or saying what he or she wants to, out of fear of negative reactions, criticism, rejection, and simply opting to avoid social situations instead."

Wikipedia

"Shyness is the tendency to feel awkward, worried or tense during social encounters, especially with unfamiliar people. Severely shy people may have physical symptoms like blushing, sweating, a pounding heart or upset stomach; negative feelings about themselves; worries about how others view them; and a tendency to withdraw from social interactions."

Encyclopedia of psychology

My stomach got upset just from reading that definition. It's so vivid and to the point. As is this one, from Free Dictionary's <u>Medical Dictionary</u>:

"Brain activity is one component of shyness ... This may cause the person to blush, tense up, or start sweating. Those are some reactions caused when the brain signals its warning. The person may avoid eye contact, look down, become very quiet, or fumble over words."

As you can see, shyness is fully connected with social encounters. It's an internal trait, but only influences you in social situations. It doesn't trouble you very much when you are alone.

Shyness defines, or rather constrains, your ability to interact with others, especially with strangers. When a shy person approaches an unfamiliar person, her brain starts to send its unpleasant and distracting warnings. It's hard to focus on social rituals and conversation when your heart is pounding so hard you're worried you'll have a stroke.

For me, it was upset stomach; the uneasiness of it near-indescribable, so strong as to almost be painful. My hands would shake and my breathing would quicken. I couldn't gather my thoughts to say something relevant, let alone witty. Oh, and I had a lump in my throat. Why did none of the "expert" definitions mention this? Do you know how hard it is to say something coherently and confidently with a lump in the throat?! Yeah, good luck!

Each encounter was torturous.

Of course, there are varying degrees of shyness, varying symptoms, but it's never comfortable.

After each encounter, I suffered the sting of defeat. I would relive the experience in my imagination, pointing out every faux pas, every awkward line, and every time I could have given a better answer to a question. I beat myself up, called myself stupid, awkward and unsociable. I worried that every new person I met would immediately see these traits and label me. Each experience drove the painful spike of shyness deeper.

The Roots of Confidence

The word confidence comes from the Latin *com* – "with," and *fidere* – "to trust." Modern definitions mildly convey this root meaning, but tend to skirt the core of it in our success-oriented society. Confidence now means:

- a feeling or belief that you can do something well or succeed at something
- a feeling or belief that someone or something is good or has the ability to succeed at something

- a feeling of self-assurance arising from an appreciation of one's own abilities or qualities
- a feeling of being certain that something will happen or that something is true
- faith or belief that one will act in a right, proper, or effective way
- a feeling that things will go well, but also a judgment on our own or others' abilities.

Confidence is a multidimensional concept, so it isn't used much in psychology. Other terms are used to describe some of this: self-esteem (feelings about your self-worth), self-efficacy (feelings about your competence in relation to achievements, goals and life events) or optimism (the tendency to believe that one will generally experience good versus bad outcomes in life). They all focus on the internal meaning of confidence, not the part of the psyche that refers to judgments and beliefs about others.

Jim Rohn defines confidence a bit differently than psychologists, a definition derived from the etymology of the word. The meaning Rohn finds in the word confidence is much closer to the definition of confidence used in economics. Economists use a few metrics and terms related to confidence such as:

Consumer Confidence - a measure of the level of optimism consumers have about the performance of the economy.

Business Confidence - an economic indicator that measures the amount of optimism or pessimism that business managers feel about the prospects of their companies/ organizations.

These all stem from trust.

Rohn considered confidence one of the most elusive and misunderstood traits. It seems to be very self-centered, but he argued that "it is found to a greater degree in what we give to others than in what we have within or about ourselves." According to Rohn, "confidence has to do with inspiring trust," it's more of a social, than a personal trait.

Only when you feel trust can you act with trust. If you can state that you interact with new people trustingly, then you can freely state that you are a confident person and are no longer shy.

Confidence: you trust yourself to not be a jerk. You trust that the strangers you approach will be helpful, caring and supportive, rather than harmful.

You can build confidence. It's a character trait, and as such, it can be developed. I know it's hard to believe, especially if you are shy or if you've tried in the past and failed time after time.

In this way, you are similar to a little kid, who can't believe that he will learn to read one day. It seems overwhelming for that kiddo to acquire the skills and knowledge needed to master the art of reading. He needs to learn the letters, join them into words, build sentences out of them and comprehend their meaning. At the start, all these concepts are foreign.

But, nearly everybody is able to learn reading by following the educational systems developed over the centuries. The same goes with confidence. You may not be able to act confidently right now, but numerous people have developed confidence out of shyness and you are not so different from them.

Success comes from building confidence through new methods, a new perspective. Just ditch the old ideas; they weren't helpful in the past and won't be in the future.

The methods I describe in this book are not very different than the natural process of building confidence.

So, what are the natural sources of confidence?

First is your knowledge. You know that people are social creatures; it's normal for us to interact with each other. I assume you are not a psychopath, and you have some social bonds already established. Whether it's people in your family, at work or in your religious congregation, you were able to connect with other people.

You are intellectually aware of the fact that society is not seeking to harm or destroy you; 99.99 percent of the time, the worst thing that can happen to you from strangers is indifference.

Another source of confidence is the faith others have in you. If you were shy as a kid, I bet your parents encouraged you many times to attempt to play with other children. I do it all the time to my oldest son, who prefers playing on the computer over playing with his peers. When I encourage him to play with friends, it doesn't stem from my frustration about his social anxiety. Rather, it's the expression of my belief that he is perfectly capable of successful relationships; that he has the right to be confident in himself; that his own unique traits are not obstacles to connecting with others, but assets.

It's normal, natural, for people to cooperate. Every person that tries to interact with you – family member, friend, colleague or the person on the street asking you for directions – expresses the belief that you are a part of human race and, as such, are capable of social communication.

Your experience can also be a source of confidence. You are alive! That means you have already gathered the necessary life experience to interact with other people. No human is a lonely island. In fact, loneliness drives people crazy.

Confidence and shyness seem to be two poles of the same trait.

Confidence is the trust you put in yourself and, consequently, in others. Shyness is insecurity, a lack of trust in your abilities, fear you won't be socially accepted. You embody and communicate these feelings to others and in most cases you get what you give – not very satisfying interactions.

Every positive experience can reduce your shyness and boost your confidence. And, vice versa.

Anthony Robbins teaches about the feedback model, a model that perfectly expresses this concept. Your beliefs fuel your actions, your actions in turn fuel your experiences. Based on those experiences, your beliefs are shaped and the cycle begins once again.

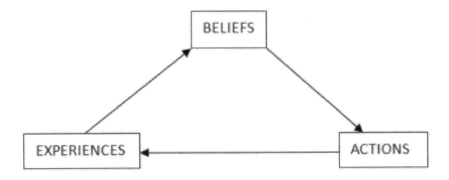

This can be a downward spiral, where your negative beliefs, fears and insecurities fuel shy actions. Those awkward attempts provide you with more experiences that 'prove' you are unworthy, a weirdo. Those experiences further enforce your beliefs.

But when you add a new component into this cycle, a new quality, it can improve your life. You can reverse the direction of that spiral. I offer you a full range of methods to do that, from the philosophy which shapes your beliefs to techniques that will add new actions and new experiences into your feedback cycle.

In conclusion: to build confidence, you need to work on trusting your abilities. But it's like the chicken-egg riddle – you don't really know which one comes first.

Trust is omnipresent in human interactions. You gained the existing trust you have in your traits thanks to your relatives, friends and other people with whom you've shared life experience. Your parents trusted that you were able to walk, talk and learn manners. Your teachers trusted that you could learn to read and write. Your friends trusted that you were cool enough to play with them. Those relationships made you who you are today.

Sadly, relationships can also be abusive and harmful and contribute to a lack of trust and confidence. But even these experiences need not define you today.

Talking to strangers is an ideal exercise to reduce your social anxiety and build your confidence. You will gain positive feedback information internally and externally. Your trust in yourself and others will fuel each other and grow simultaneously.

And it's easy.

Where Does Trust Originate?

According to Stephen R. Covey, author of the bestseller, *The 7 Habits of Highly Effective People*, trust is one of the basics of human society. Covey developed the concept of an 'emotional bank account,' which "is a metaphor that describes the amount of trust that's been built up in a relationship."

We need trust to act effectively. Imagine this situation: you are at a business conference and you are approached by a guy who wants to sell you on "a once-in-a-lifetime joint-venture business opportunity." He gives a convincing presentation. He has everything in place. His business plan is flawless; his numbers are right.

But you don't know him.

Then, replace this guy with someone familiar. You've met him at several conferences in the past few years. You cooperated on a small project which was successful. He did you a favor or two. He introduced you to the CEO of a big company in your industry that he knew personally, and, as a result, your business saw a significant revenue boost. This person you know and trust gives you the same pitch.

How would you react to his proposal? Wouldn't you be eager to jump at this joint-venture opportunity of his? Where you might have responded with skepticism to the other guy, here you respond with excitement.

Trust is such an immaterial quality, but so basic and needed wherever interactions between people take place. That's why confidence, the quality which comes 'with trust,' is such an important factor in economic models. Trust is the fabric of human society. Business life is built from infinite numbers of human interactions. Trust in others is a foundation of success.

If you want to develop confidence, you need to work on trust. Conversations with strangers are a great way to achieve this. You gradually become convinced that people are not blood-lusting beasts. They are not an alien life form acting strangely or in ways dangerous to your well-being. As soon as you emerge unscathed from a few conversations, you begin to discover that people are just like you – they look for happiness; they have good and bad days; they have the same needs and fears as you. They are eager to talk about themselves, to share their experiences or just to socialize.

All of this makes deposit after deposit into your personal "trust account." Your feeling of safety with others will grow in general. It will affect your entire life perspective.

I largely got rid of my shyness. I sometimes still feel nervous in an unfamiliar social environment, especially when approaching beautiful women I don't know. But I learned to overcome those feelings and my internal world changed dramatically.

The biggest impact has been on my daily commute. I travel about four hours every day by train and bus; 90 percent of my interactions with strangers are while traveling to and from work.

I used to ignore the people around me. At best, I thought of them as a part of the environment. When I had a bad day, I perceived them as a threat.

Now I treat my traveling compatriots like a group of friends. I've already talked to dozens of them, and exchanged smiles with many more. I am no longer indifferent to them. I look forward to my daily commute with a pinch of positive anticipation every day: "Who will I meet?" An old friend? Someone outgoing? Someone overwhelmed with problems that I could encourage with a kind word? My commute has transformed from daily struggle to daily adventure.

Indifference – The Core of Shyness

How Indifference Drives Shyness
I don't know about you, but in my case, indifference was a big factor in my social anxiety. I had no occasion to gain trust through interactions with unfamiliar people, because I hadn't been interacting with them. By doing so, I was disassociating myself from a source of trust I could otherwise use.

The foremost reason for my indifference was complacency. I'm an introvert. I don't need many relationships to function. I'm quite happy being alone most of the time. I built several close relationships, but did not spread my net far. My family is my unrelenting source of support, soaking me with all the love and trust I need. In my mind, the price of being outgoing was just too high to bother.

So I stayed in my comfort zone. Sure, there were a few times of discomfort, like seeing the boy with cancer. But 99 percent of the time, I felt OK with myself, and I didn't need to spend any additional effort to achieve this.

Modern society strongly supports such attitudes. The number of personal relationships an ordinary person needs to function in society is the lowest in the history of this planet. In an era where you can order groceries, manage your bank account and send people gifts online, it's nearly possible to exist only interacting through technology. You can restrict the number of people in your tribe to the closest family, neighbors and colleagues.

There are people who have lived in their apartments for years and don't recognize their neighbors. There are people who work remotely, whose best approximation of work relationships is a Skype call. There are emigrants who see their families only a few weeks every year, if they see them that much.

New technologies support shrinking personal interactions. They make life easier, but they make it also less sociable. Take, for example, the virtual shopping cart – it is a vehicle of economic trust. You don't need to trust the guy with the small website very much as long as he is connected with ClickBank, which guarantees your money back if you are not satisfied with the product or service you receive.

The main goal of technology is to make life easier and perform daily tasks more efficiently. It does this job very well, but it robs you of the small opportunities to bond with others.

Technology also stepped boldly into the world of entertainment. Video games, movies, television: all are amazingly effective in eating our time alive. I know something about this – I'm a computer game addict.

Though I have largely curbed the problem, it is something that used to eat up a great deal of time that could be used for more enriching pursuits. Even as an adult with my many occupations – father, husband, church community member and employee with a three- to four-hour commute – I was still able to play more than 24 hours of Civilization IV in a month.

Games are everywhere. Mobile devices are more popular with each passing year, and now you can carry your own entertainment center with you. It is easier than ever to be distracted at any time, day or night, at home or on the go.

Nowadays, you have access to the whole world, but at the same time, the whole world also has access to you. It seems like everybody wants your attention: political parties vying for your vote; activist movements who want you to support their cause; charities who count on your generosity; and companies who want your money. If your firewall is not raised very high, if you haven't cut yourself off from these unwanted messages, you are exposed to a myriad of communication, and each one eats a piece of your attention and your time.

In effect, you have less time and attention for the people around you. All of those attention thieves make you more indifferent. These attention thieves alienate you further from strangers, makes them seem even further outside 'your tribe.' What is left of your time, you give to the close circle of people you know very well – usually your family and colleagues.

British anthropologist Robin Dunbar concluded that humans don't really treat other individuals as part of their race. According to him, we are only able to be close to a specific number of people. These people are a part of our 'tribe.' Called Dunbar's Number, he estimated it to be between 100 and 250. The rest of humanity outside this circle are unknown to us – inhuman.

Dunbar's conclusions have been readily accepted by the public at large. When I first heard of them, I was nodding in agreement. They seem to perfectly describe our reality. That's how our brains work: we really try to comprehend this complicated world of ours. In doing so, our brain filters and simplifies the billions of stimuli we get. As a result, we alienate people with whom we don't interact closely or often.

But is it possible to change that? Absolutely! You are the one who allowed time thieves and entertainment to hijack your attention. You can also reverse the process. The more I practice personal development, the more I believe that all we need to change are our attention and the uses of our time.

My Dunbar number was very low and I was consciously avoiding adding anyone else into my inner circle. But, daily practice and conscious effort to expand my comfort zone has changed this.

If shutting others out is so damaging and limiting to ourselves, why do we do it? Because you and I love ease. We are programmed to take an easy path. If you were to consciously process even 10 percent of the signals you get via your senses, you would collapse from information overload in no time. The brain tends to put everything not crucial to your survival in background mode. This includes your fellow human beings. It's so much easier to become indifferent than it is to sustain an extensive network of relationships. It's easier to touch your tablet or mobile phone than to touch another person.

Let's take, for example, the 'Like' feature on Facebook. It's very easy to click and make the other person aware that you saw her message and reacted positively to it. It's an order of magnitude easier than saying, "Thank you." in the comment section, or – God forbid! – explaining how the message made you feel or think.

394 likes and only 3 comments

We love ease of communication. But is it really easier to be dependent on those tools than to learn how to interact with people? You use them because, deep inside, you love to communicate. That's why social media sites are so popular. They made forming and maintaining relationships ridiculously easy. It's extremely comforting to use them. It is alarming.

However, Jim Rohn states that the easiest things in life are the least profitable. I agree with him. It seems like everything that is easy and rewarding in the short term is difficult and unfulfilling in the long term. The opposite is also true. What is hard and unrewarding in the short term will become easy and fulfilling in the long term.

We don't pay attention to what's easy. In the long term, the use of these tools and systems leads to alienation. You will ignore people around you; your brain will put them in the background.

The real enemy of your transformation is not the companies who want your attention or the games which steal your time. The real enemy is you, because it's you who allowed them to do so. Without your cooperation, they wouldn't steal your time and attention.

This indifference to human relationships is crippling you. It's crippling our society. Stephen Covey wrote that low interpersonal trust increases the overall friction in any kind of cooperation. You focus on protecting your *status quo* instead of throwing yourself fully into the job at hand.

What You Stand to Lose Through Shyness

Let's talk about a simple thing like asking for directions. If you are lost, it's obvious that locals can guide you quickly and effectively. One time, GPS guided me into the heart of a forest. I was looking for the highway. I stopped to ask for directions and the locals showed me a shortcut which I would never have found in the electronic database of GPS, a road to the backyard of a gas station near the highway.

The common opinion is that reluctance to ask for directions stems from a macho complex. I think it's just an uneasiness about talking to strangers.

Low confidence can cost you not only emotionally, but financially, too. There is a story in *Chicken Soup for the Soul* about a couple who wanted to attend a seminar in another state. Unfortunately, they had very little money. They called various people and institutions, asking for help until they got everything they needed – the plane tickets, seminar tickets, accommodations, meals and a rental car.

I've had similar experiences. My publishing career has been made possible because I asked for help. My English is mediocre at best. When I finished my first manuscript, I posted it on a Facebook community centered around personal growth, and asked for help. There, I found a noble soul who helped me edit my book. I can't imagine what would have happened if I didn't have that help; it's possible I would have quit then and there.

I made some connections in a Facebook authors' group and got the covers for all my books done for free. For my previous book, "Master Your Time in 10 Minutes a Day," my editor offered me free editing and marketing services. It made such a difference that my royalties were 15 times higher in February 2014 than in the previous month. To ask for a favor, you need some level of confidence and you have to overcome your shyness. If you won't initiate the interaction, nothing will happen.

You often need some level of existing 'Emotional Bank Account' deposits in advance, which means you have working relationships in place before you ask for help. For that, you need to be able to start and sustain relationships.

When I organized my time management book launch, I reached out and asked for help from fellow bloggers; 100 percent of those with whom I had prior relationships agreed to support me. Only 8 percent of those bloggers (two dozen or so) who didn't know me before gave me some real help.

Work on yourself in advance, before you need these relationships. You have to agree to a small level of discomfort to grow, to overcome your shyness and develop your confidence. The cost of avoiding strangers now may not seem very high – your social life is just a little poorer – but the opportunity cost may be huge. Develop your social skills before you really need them.

I preferred not to notice people around me and spent my time in my internal world. I felt safer that way. However, it was a colossal mistake, because of my self-talk. Do you know who talks to you most often?

You do. You and yourself have an endless conversation going in your head. It can be interrupted by external events, tasks or interactions, but as soon as you are left alone, you immediately go back to it. If you are like 95 percent of people, most of what you tell yourself is negative crap.

I was guilty as hell of it. I'm my own worst enemy. When I began my downward spiral of self-criticism, I used very rude vocabulary. I had no mercy on myself.

Unless you live in the most abject part of society, no one else is talking to you in more humiliating words than you are. I don't know any other human being who says worse things to me or about me than what I have in my own mind. I don't think I'm much different, in that regard, from others.

And you prefer this conversation over talking to strangers? You think that's more attractive than the "danger" of being vulnerable? That's a poor choice.

I've talked to dozens of strangers and the worst that happened to me was indifference. I buttonholed one man about the book he was reading and all he answered was, "Well, it's not very interesting." He just wasn't in the mood for a chat.

Compare that with my internal self-talk:

"C'mon, you jerk, talk to the guy! He won't bite you (I suppose)."

"Ha, ha, very funny. I know he won't bite me, you dunce, but what if he rejects me?"

"Oh, c'mon, don't be a weenie, talk to him!"

And then, after the stranger's answer, "You see, all my effort for no good! He didn't want to talk, booo!"

"And he was right, who would want to talk to such a loser?! Pshaw!"

All that the stranger expressed, in a very neutral way, was his unwillingness to chat, but at the same time, I experienced a whole lot of abuse from myself.

We tend to be very harsh toward ourselves. I wouldn't bear anybody else talking to me in such a way, but I do when it comes from within. Anytime I talk to strangers, I hear a majority of nice things. Their speech is always more civilized than my internal dialog.

I should certainly prefer their company over my own.

Success Through a New Philosophy

To Each His Own

Everyone has a personal philosophy. Some people, like Gandhi, are conscious enough to have it written down and clearly stated. Others are unaware of it, but they still live according to their set of rules. For example: "I love the couch, beer and TV above all else." Jim Rohn, a self-made millionaire, was convinced that personal philosophy determines almost every outcome in an individual's life. It's not hard to agree with him. Just compare Gandhi's accomplishments to those of the "couch & TV" philosophy.

Rohn also believed that every individual is capable of shaping his own philosophy. After all, he was able to shape his successful philosophy out of early failure. He was a miserable and broken young man with gloomy prospects ahead. He worked for six years, only to find himself deep in debt and with few options. Then he changed his philosophy ... and his life.

My own experience follows Rohn's. As soon as I changed my philosophy, I began seeing different outcomes in my life. My way of thinking was transformed, so was my weight, my bank account, my reading skills, my career, and many other things.

Nobody can impose his philosophy on you. I won't even try. All I can do is to show you mine and encourage you to pick out elements which are in accordance with your values. I call it The Ten-Minute Philosophy. At its core is: "I KNOW that daily, sustained action brings results."

It has some additional rules such as:

- The action can be of minuscule size and still bring you closer to your goal.
- Do not do anything against your goal, because then your "daily sustained action" becomes directed against your purpose.

This philosophy triumphs over two major obstacles to any change: fear of failure and premature abandonment of your efforts. I encourage you to check out the full scope of my philosophy, because it drives results.

Below, I emphasize the elements which are directly connected with speaking to strangers.

10 Minutes to Conquer Fear

In my experience, this was a big factor sabotaging my efforts to approach strangers. I was paralyzed by fear. My hands shook, my voice trembled, my stomach convulsed. But when you KNOW that, in the end, you will be able to do it, there is nothing to fear. The outcome is already determined. It may take you some time, and there will probably be some setbacks, but the result will be visible from the beginning.

You don't have to believe that you will achieve your goal. It's not mandatory. Doubts and hesitations are not welcome, but they also won't torpedo your plans as long as you stick to The Ten-Minute Philosophy.

I can vouch for this approach. I didn't believe I could be a successful writer. I had no experience, no skills, I had never written for a broad audience before.

But I consistently did what successful authors do – I wrote and wrote, edited, wrote, corrected, wrote, published and wrote some more. I've sold more than 2,500 copies of my books and given more than 14,000 copies away during free promotions. By February 2014, my book royalties equaled 50 percent of my 9 to 5 salary. I didn't believe in this outcome from the start; I just consistently did the small daily actions.

(Not) Giving Up

The normal cycle with any new venture goes like this:

1. You decide to change.
2. You are scared of the change, but determined to do it.
3. You start.
4. You hit a wall.
5. You 'fail.'

This almost always happens at the beginning. You don't really know what to do; you lack skills and/or knowledge. You are destined to struggle at first. After the first failure, your doubts start to raise their ugly heads. You try again; you fail again. Your doubts get stronger; your resolve gets weakened. You lose your enthusiasm for the change and your efforts from this point are half-hearted. Half-hearted attempts have even less likelihood of succeeding, so you fail again and your negative attitude is reinforced.

Then, you give up. That's the normal cycle. Because of it, only 8% of people are successful in achieving their New Year's resolutions.

How does the Ten-Minute Philosophy deal with that? It breaks the cycle before it takes root. Your doubts won't stop your actions; you simply do the action consistently – no matter what – because you know it's going to give you the results you seek. You are running a marathon. It may be tough, but you have to run or you will never reach the finish line. You know this, so you keep running.

It all sounds too good to be true, right? Well, hang with me, because it gets even better. I said before that a personal philosophy cannot be imposed on you. It doesn't need to be; the beauty of this philosophy is that it has already worked in your life. You have already used it and seen results.

All you need to make this philosophy your own is to find it at work in your past experiences. Take a moment to think of any successful area of your life. It can be anything – your marriage, a specific skill, your career, the fact you have never had a car accident, good grades at school, your great relationship with your parents, etc. The best example for this exercise will be something that you take for granted, but that other people praise you for.

So, pick one and think: what makes me successful in this area? What's the difference between me and the people who praise me for this? Chances are, they are less successful at it. What do I do that they don't? I bet you will find some sustained action underlying your success.

If you look, you will find examples of how this philosophy has already manifested in your own life. Embrace it and you will see the way it changes your daily actions – and your life.

I conceived this concept when I thought about my small successes and experiences – the love in my family, receiving a scholarship at university, my fitness results (more than 100 consecutive pushups). I found a tiny sustained activity behind each of them.

The Ten-Minute Philosophy works in both directions. A tiny sustained action can lead you to undesired results, too. Perhaps you are obese because you eat fast food every day. While one fast food meal certainly won't make you obese, the cumulative effects of eating like that every day will. I was overweight because I ate sweets every day and vegetables only occasionally. However, I don't recommend dwelling on this side of things when you try embracing your personal philosophy; it can be disheartening.

The Mindset of a Confident Person

Your Mindset is Crucial
We tend to belittle the impact of right-thinking on our actions. We are all for, well ... action. I bet that since beginning this book you have been thinking, "All right, all right, but what do I have to do to be more confident?!"

Let's look at the definition of shyness once again:

"Shyness is the tendency to feel awkward, worried or tense during social encounters, especially with unfamiliar people. Severely shy people may have physical symptoms like blushing, sweating, a pounding heart or upset stomach; negative feelings about themselves; worries about how others view them; and a tendency to withdraw from social interactions."

Shyness (and confidence) starts in your head. The emotions are the bedrock, from which results physical symptoms, which then leads to action (or lack of action).

If you are a hardcore realist and dismiss affirmations and visualizations out of hand as woo-woo, it may be time to get real with yourself.

When I was researching self-talk for this book, guess what Google came up with most? The answer is one I wouldn't have guessed in a million years – sports performance. Where some focus on training methods and intervals, the equipment and other material factors, top performers focus on self-talk.

Our society is so deeply materialistic that we ignore the truth, we forget that everything we do starts in our heads. Scientists cannot measure everything in the human brain. They work hard and discover new things every day, but our knowledge of the brain remains the tip of the iceberg. We know how the atoms connect to create complicated chemical structures, but we don't really know how our brain works. It breeds a lot of confusion, and to avoid this confusion we choose to focus on the material side of things. We esteem "how" over "why."

Don't get me wrong. Action is great. It always wins over inaction. Doers always have an advantage over pure thinkers (or talkers). But, to act consistently over a long period of time, doers need some underlying philosophy that drives action. Having it, they don't overthink their actions. Even if they think too little, and are unprepared for obstacles, they reap the rewards of action by acting and failing forward. Without such a philosophy, they would fall into the cycle of giving up, as described in the previous chapter.

Mindset is crucial; it's a key to your success.

Mental exercises

To work on your mindset, you need mental exercises. They are great for the shy person, because they don't require them to actually go through the stress of approaching and talking to strangers. Start in your head.

Do you know the definition of madness? "Doing the same things over and over and expecting different results." You have to try something else if you want to progress, even if it feels woo-woo, illogical, or naive.

Flex Those Muscles

What is the Muscle Testing Technique? Will I have to put on workout clothes and get sweaty? No. While the gym can be a great place to meet people, in this application, Muscle Testing Technique is just another name for using your imagination. Everyone has an imagination. Just like breathing, no one had to teach you how to do it; it is a natural, inborn ability all humans have.

The only problem I had with using this technique was that, at first, my imagination was so rusty that it was difficult to apply to overcoming my shyness. Once I realized that it was possible and I began applying it, it was a piece of cake.

Another obstacle you might come up against is the internal resistance to using 'new-agey' techniques. It's downright scary what kind of websites and mystical language spring up in Google when you search for "muscle testing technique."

I overcame my shyness because I was desperate to change my life. The skeptics had no answers for me. All they had to say was, "Live your life as it is and hope it doesn't get worse." Frankly, I couldn't pinpoint which of the more mystical or "new-agey" approaches helped me most. I simultaneously tried a LOT of different things. I was desperate to change my life – I was not looking to perform scientific research, giving each method a six-month trial and carefully plotting the results before switching to another. But even this unfocused approach helped me; I got the results I was looking for.

Don't be afraid of trying new things at the risk of feeling like an idiot afterward. Nobody sees you when you do this. After all, it's your imagination; it's in your head.

I also think that part of this resistance is just a subconscious inertia. Your brain loves the existing *status quo* and hates any changes. Using your imagination to solve problems seems like too much work. Your mind prefers to numb itself with a hefty dose of TV or video games.

Having said all of the above – simply using my imagination has helped me enormously and the results were almost instant.

The actual process is very simple. You don't need any special time or environment to do it. It won't hurt to have several minutes of peace and quiet, but it's not necessary.

Begin with visualizing the situation that causes you discomfort. As this book focuses on talking to strangers, I advise you to imagine yourself approaching someone you don't know. The more vividly you can see the details, the better. Therefore, imagine the specific person who you are shy around.

I should mention here that this technique is not really about visualizing the result. The sole reason for imagining yourself in this stressful situation is to elicit the uneasy feelings in your body – the butterflies in your stomach, a lump in your throat, etc. Any thought or picture in your mind which causes these physical reactions is good enough.

Once you are in this uneasy place, focus your attention, your mind, your awareness on it. There's no special technique here; you will know when you have mentally connected with your body's state.

Focus on these uneasy sensations in your body and embrace them. They are part of you, the reactions of your own body. At first, don't try to have a dialog with these feelings or force them to change. Just be mindful of them; recognize them the same way you would recognize the sensation of a breeze on your skin.

Once you are aware of the sensations, ask your body: where do they come from? Why this tension? Why do I feel this way? Direct those questions at the unpleasant sensations, not to your body in general. You don't need to ask them all at once or in any specific order. They are just prompts for starting the conversation. Pick the question which most directly applies to your circumstances.

Once you begin the dialog, listen to your body's answers. Don't argue with them. Don't get mad at them. Just listen to them. Also, don't expect instant enlightenment. Simply start the dialog, something like:

You: "Why this tension?"

Body: "I'm afraid."

You: "What are you afraid of?"

Body: "I'm afraid of this person." (The answers come from your subconscious which is not the brightest part of your psyche.)

You: "Why are you afraid of her?"

Body: "Because she is attractive and I'm not."

Continue the dialog, and work it until you find the root of the problem. It's a left-brain activity driven by intuition, I can't guide you to your specific solution with hypothetical dialog. But to continue the example above, you could ask why you think you are unattractive or why the disparity in perceived attractiveness is holding you back.

Just keep listening. Your subconscious is quite dumb. It uses various excuses to stop you from getting into hot water. When revealed, the "reasons" may seem to be silly. Silly or not, they are the reasons that keep you from talking to strangers.

Sometimes, such interrogation can lead you to your early life. You know, psychologists are not just a bunch of ignorant eggheads. There are genuine causes and conditions from your childhood that shape your adult behaviors. However, it is important to remember that these factors can be changed with sustained effort; they are not immutable.

The most important part of this process? Not to back off.

These images you call up, these sensations in your body, these answers you receive, are not likely to be pleasant. Going through them will cause you discomfort – this means you are doing it correctly. But facing them consciously makes all the difference.

You will stop reacting to those impulses and, instead, will interact with them. No longer will they drive you like lines of code drive a robot. You will suddenly find yourself with the ability to input your own pieces of code.

Once you start, don't stop. There is no single right way to do it right – there is only your way.

When I was introduced to this technique for the first time, it was a variant which didn't need words. There is a primal nature to it, more basic even than language. The crucial part of the Muscle Testing Technique is to call upon the images, sensations and thoughts you have when you try to approach a new person, and to embrace those thoughts, to replace your automatic impulses with conscious effort to understand what's going on.

I used the technique for the first time while doing my morning workout. I used a guided recording; the exercise itself took about five minutes, with roughly 10 more minutes of introductions and explanations.

At first, it all seemed a little bit "out there." The recording I used was about cooperating with your own fears. When the trainer asked me to visualize something I was afraid of, I thought about talking to strangers. At the time, all I could do was smile shyly at strangers. I didn't yet know how to overcome my fears and take these interactions to the next level.

But, thinking about the tension in my body ... how was that supposed to help me?

Despite my doubts, I did the exercises. I was a complete novice, but I repeated it the very same day while on a train to work. I remember I was sitting across from a lady I wanted to talk to. I came up with some compliment to start a conversation but, as usual, I was getting nervous.

I targeted the uneasy feeling in my stomach and embraced it in my mind. I don't remember if I chickened out that time, but I vividly remember the experience of consciously stopping the fear cycle and pondering it. For the first time, I wasn't simply reacting to the impulses in my subconscious mind and body, now I was now responding to them with my conscious mind.

That was my breakthrough moment. Regardless of whether I was actually able to begin a conversation in that moment, I was soon able to open my mouth and start meeting new people.

I'll repeat this to drive the point home: you don't need professional help to make this change; you don't need to practice it a lot; you don't need to do it exactly how I describe it or even believe that it works to get started.

Just. Do. It.

Attention and Appreciation – Beating Indifference

Another way to practice your social skills without leaving your mind is the simple act of thinking about people around you. From time to time, turn off your internal dialog, take a look around and recognize others. Give them your attention and mental energy.

This is the first step in initiating a successful relationship. You can't approach other people if you are full of yourself and thinking only about your motives and needs. Such self-centered attitudes are the cornerstone of the shyness curse; they drive you to think mostly about yourself – "I am not good enough. I am such a failure. What will this person think or say about me ... "

Indifference was a big part of my problem with talking to strangers. Dunbar's theory has merit; strangers are a bit like alien creatures. My imagination was making up impossible stories about them, just like a kid's imagination populating her wardrobe with monsters.

This exercise makes you more open toward other people. Remember what Jim Rohn said: you can't feel confident in yourself unless you put your confidence in others. To begin, you need to simply recognize their existence, and not just as part of your landscape. You must see the person as another human being with the same complicated world of thoughts and emotions boiling inside them.

So, who should you recognize? Everyone. Whether is it the "hot chick," the homeless guy, the old, obese lady or the man who looks like the CEO of a Fortune 500 company, you should give them the same attention. Essentially, we are all the same. We are hungry inside for attention and love.

Once again, it's not a bad idea to make this a meditation exercise. Sit in isolation, close your eyes, relax, recall a few people you met that day and ponder them. The more attention, time and effort you put into your practices, the better the results.

The great thing about this exercise is that it is so amazingly flexible. You can do it in five seconds, while running to the bus stop. It works for everyone, even the busiest person in the midst of bustle or turmoil.

Small consistency always wins over massive but inconsistent action. I assume you believe you are simply too busy to spend half of your day on various mental exercises; however, building a habit of recognizing people around you will eventually show you that you do have the mental space to do just that. These exercises have a compound effect and will become second nature with practice.

You can practice anywhere – on a bus or train, while driving through traffic, in the mall, at work, or events, or while on a walk. Wherever there are people around you, you can exercise this part of your psyche. It's an ideal "filler" – an activity you can do while doing other, more physical tasks.

Step one: acknowledge people around you.

Stop thinking about your business for a moment. Look around you, find a person you don't know and give him or her a thought.

If you don't suspend your internal dialog, if you don't raise your head and take a look around, it won't happen. That's the minimal commitment you have to undertake.

Step two: think about that person.

The bottom line is to think anything positive. When you have just a single moment, it's enough to stop and think about their image: "What a unique pattern on her nails," or "He has strong hands," or "This kid's cheeks are so cute," maybe "I like that jacket," or "What an interesting dress."

Your task is to get closer to the people, not alienate them further in your mind. Focus on finding in them something you can appreciate; something which will make them more human in your eyes. Two methods I have successfully used are to find the common denominator between us, or something I can appreciate about them.

Next time you notice the homeless guy and think: "Whoa! He smells worse than I do after an intense workout," you aren't improving the situation. Instead, confront that negativity and decide to think something like: "What hardship he endures every day; he must be a tough guy!"

The same goes for the other extreme, too. For example, if you see an attractive person and think,

"Wow, I would do (insert sexual thought here) with him/her if I had the chance," you are dehumanizing that person. They become just a sexual object in your mind, not a fellow human being. When I see an attractive woman on a 5 a.m. train, I have trained myself to recognize her in admiration, rather than lust: "Wow, she put in a lot of effort to look her best so early in the day."

Be specific, impart them with human traits. Instead of thinking "Wow, that's one hot chick," think, "She seems to place a priority on taking care of herself."

As for the common denominator thing? Well, I simply try to find anything we have in common. If I notice someone with a kid, I immediately relate to them, because I'm a parent, too. When I see a rebellious teenager, I can relate to him, too; in my teens, I had long, greasy hair and a backpack with symbols and slogans scrawled in pen.

Because I'm a reader at my core, I can relate to anyone who reads, whether it's a magazine, an e-book or a paperback. The first thing I appreciate in every reader is their drive for self-improvement. Every kind of reading is valuable in my eyes.

If you struggle to find commonality with others, think of the subjects you are passionate about, the topics which are easy and natural for you. Write them down. Include them in your visualizations.

Step three: praise others in your mind.

This is the natural extension of the previous steps. You noticed someone, you found what you appreciate in them and then you imagine starting the conversation with them by giving this praise.

From here, I find it easy to go beyond the visualization in my exercises. It's far easier to imagine myself saying, "I admire the loving patience you have for your kid. I'm a parent myself and I know what it takes," than saying "Excuse me lady, you have nice, slender legs." And it is easier to put it into practice later on.

This all may sound intimidating, but I assure you that after just a few days of practice, you will find yourself doing this instinctively. Each instance of the exercise will take you just a moment, but the results will be astounding!

Visualizing Success

Another method of employing your imagination in developing your confidence is visualization. I'm someone who can hardly recall his mother's face in his mind. I'm sure my visualization skills are among the poorest on this planet. And yet, even I successfully used it on my quest to talk with strangers.

Because you are likely already better at visualization than I am, I will not give a comprehensive course in visualization here. I will teach you just the basics; the techniques I successfully used.

Again, you don't need a perfect meditation environment or 30 minute sessions to do it. Any place and time where your mind is free to think will do the trick, like while walking or working out.

At the core of the method I used – envisioning the conversation in my head, pretending that I am talking to a stranger. Imagine approaching someone and starting a conversation. If you have a vivid imagination and an 'avatar' – for example, someone from your neighborhood you would like to talk to, but feel too shy – then imagine that specific person. Visualization works better if you give your brain some convincing details. Just like a movie – if the acting is poor, it's hard to engage in the story. If the movie is good and the acting convincing, you are more inclined to believe it.

However, the key to visualization is emotion. The more positive emotions you foster, the more effective this exercise will be.

So, imagine that the stranger responds enthusiastically to your attempt to start a conversation. At your first words, he lights up and gives you a big smile. Imagine feeling at ease and enjoying the experience. Your visualization should include all the qualities you want to possess and express in your interactions with others – wit, confidence, firmness, sympathy – whatever it is that you pursue. Exchange a few sentences with the imaginary stranger, focusing on those qualities and trying to actually stir them up within yourself.

I recommend doing this exercise multiple times a day and always keeping it short, say under a minute. Do it while walking to the bus stop, in line at the cafeteria or while among strangers when you feel unable to start a conversation. Pick one person from the crowd and imagine initiating conversation with her.

This exercise has an additional advantage. Many times when you start it, your internal critic will turn on and try to meddle. That's what you want. It will allow you to get to know his arguments. As I said earlier, they are usually very weak. Once you hear what he is saying, you will be able to ridicule him, to shut his arguments down.

You can do this by altering the course of your imaginative conversation. For example, you say "Hi" to an attractive woman. Your internal critic chips in and the woman answers in the manner you are most afraid of – she screams: "Help me! This pervert is bothering me!"

Just by recognizing this vision, you realize how irrational this trepidation is. Then you can alter the situation asking with concern: "Where is he? I'll protect you from him!"

When my internal critic imposes on my visualization like that, I prefer to ridicule him using my imagination. So, in my mind, I add cartoon attributes to the woman's panic – her eyes get huge, her jaw drops on the floor and her long hair stands on end.

Using this technique, you transform a feeling of discomfort into a feeling of joy. The critic's job is to warn you and make you feel uneasy. He is a serious guy and has a hard time being ridiculed. He usually backs off for good after such a treatment.

I should mention, this is not my invention. This technique is one of the elements used in Logotherapy, the psychotherapy school of thought created by Viktor Frankl.

Another advantage of visualization is that you exercise a conscious control over your mind and internal dialog. This is handy in just about everything. Every second you spend consciously is a second taken away from your autopilot, whose priorities are usually a bit different (typically: comfort, comfort and comfort at any price, here and now!).

I have personally found short, specific visualizations much easier than any advanced forms. As I mentioned before, my imagination isn't the best. Pictures in my mind are usually static, fuzzy and monochromatic. It takes a lot of effort for me to sustain any vivid image in my mind for more than five seconds. I cannot even envision my biggest dreams coming true!

But, this exercise is as much about the conversation as it is about images. The person I talk to is static, monochromatic and fuzzy, but the actual lines are clearly audible and the conversation flows uninterrupted. And I effortlessly stir up positive responses inside my mind and body.

These exercises work. If they don't directly build your confidence, at least they act as a vaccine against your internal critic.

Hard Work Pays Off – Techniques for Conquering Shyness

The 5 Stages of Conversation for the Chronically Shy

I found this guide to the stages of conversation by doing a search online:

1. Opening
2. Introduction
3. Find common ground
4. Keep it going
5. Wrap it up

I think it's an excellent summary of what's really happening during a normal chat. But if you lack the confidence to start the conversation in the first place, such a blueprint is quite useless. You may know 40 excellent opening lines by heart, but if you don't have the courage to say any of them, they won't help you.

So, I modified the model slightly, according to my experiences:

1. Opening

You need to muster your courage before you actually talk to a stranger. If I open my mouth, 80 percent of the job is already done. The rest is easy. When you are shy, the opening itself isn't a problem, because you simply don't open up. You don't approach the other person; you don't start the conversation.

Get yourself together and decide to start the conversation.

2. Introduction

Your first line may be important and lead the whole conversation to its final destination. Or, it may not. So don't put too much weight on it. You should mention some common experience or trait in your opening line, building the foundation for the next stage.

3. Find Common Ground

Ask questions. People love to talk about themselves or give their opinions. Look for what I call "a common denominator" – something you both share – a common characteristic, story, interest or experience.

4. Keep it going

Give your feedback or opinion about their remarks and ask more questions relevant to the topics already discussed.

5. Wrap it up

Finish the conversation with grace. Show appreciation by saying something like, "I really enjoyed our conversation." Or you can reflect back on the highlights to show that you were a good listener, such as, "Well, keep up the good work on your drawing project."

As you can see, I skipped the introductory stage. In my culture, it's not common to start the conversation with small talk and a personal introduction ("What lovely weather today, isn't it? I'm Michal"). When I gave it some thought, I realized that I have never introduced myself in a conversation with a stranger, but it has worked very well in my case. If it's common in your culture to introduce yourself at the beginning, then by all means do so.

Preparing to Talk to Others – Passive Exercises

Let's talk about enormously helpful techniques that are accessible to nearly everyone. With the exception of people with certain actual handicaps, anyone can use these powerful strategies. Their usefulness lies in their passive nature. You don't need the cooperation of a stranger to use them. They all simply depend on your own actions.

This is an important quality for anyone paralyzed by shyness. In my experience, I was really afraid of interaction – what would the other person think or say about me? The truth is, they will always think and say something. You can't avoid that – it's at the core of interactions and relationships. Being paralyzed by such a thought is like sitting in your car and being paralyzed by thinking about how others drivers will react to your actions on the highway. It's just irrational.

1. Make eye contact

The advantages of making eye contact with strangers are twofold. First, you exercise control over your lack of confidence; you proactively diminish your shyness. Action conquers fears. You stop thinking about your imaginary limitations and start doing something. You don't need the cooperation of the stranger to make it happen. You have control over the process. It's you who chooses the particular person and when to do it.

The second advantage is that you start to learn that people around you are not mean or harmful. I used to populate the wardrobe of my mind with monsters who mocked or attacked me.

I've looked into the eyes of hundreds, maybe even thousands, of strangers during the past 18 months. Not once has the stranger attacked me physically. Not even once have I gotten an aggressive reaction. No one has asked me angrily, "Why are you staring at me?!" For that matter, no one has asked me that politely. Not. Even. Once.

Of course, I'm not talking about approaching the stranger and getting right in his face. All you need to do is just catch someone's glance. I make eye contact all the time, on public transportation, in church, walking down the street, at cultural events ... everywhere.

Eye contact is a tiny habit which will help you to introduce big changes in your life. It's how I restarted my quest of talking to strangers. I promised myself that I would look into the eyes of a stranger at least once a day. I felt I could do at least this much. It was so easy, I couldn't miss, and in that way, I developed consistency and didn't give up on overcoming my shyness.

The results? I'm no longer a shrinking violet.

2. Smile at a stranger

The next important step in becoming sociable is using your smile. Often we are so locked in our fears and insecurities regarding others that we don't notice they have their own struggles. Our fast-paced society isolates us, and the simple act of smiling can knock down the barriers between us.

So make eye contact and smile. You will be surprised by the mix of responses you get. Some people will flinch, wince or recoil: "A stranger smiling at me? This is so unexpected!" Many people will look away to break the eye contact, plainly feeling uncomfortable. Many will look at you incredulously: "Is it real? Is this person smiling at me?" They will take a quick look around for the person you are actually smiling at, before looking back at you when they realize they are the correct recipient of your smile.

The handful that smile back at me are the ones I love best. There will be such people in your case, too. But remember, if someone looks away or winces, it is reflective more of them than of you. Perhaps they, too, would benefit from this book.

So, how is this whole smiling thing done? Well, just look someone in the eyes and then force your mouth to twist into the resemblance of smile. That's not exactly the perfect way to do it, but that's how I started. You don't do anything perfectly at the beginning. In fact, when you start any venture you are in the lowest, least-experienced point. You will never do it worse than the first time. The only way to become better at it is through practice.

I developed the habit of smiling at strangers simultaneously with the habit of looking them in the eyes. A smile is the natural progression from a look. Do it at your pace. If you feel confident enough in this already, you can start with one of the more active techniques.

3. Step it up

If you are still afraid of talking to strangers, but you feel your progress is too slow for your taste, make the challenge bigger. I started with making eye contact with a stranger at least once a day, but quickly (within a week), I aimed for making eye contact with every stranger.

I went from forcing myself to smile, to making my smile more natural. From there, I stepped it up again. I only considered the smiling exercise done when the stranger noticed me and my smile, and when he responded in some way, whether by flinching, looking away or smiling back at me.

Do the same thing over and over and over again, but do it more often and do it better.

It's Go Time! – Talking to Others

These techniques build on your progress from the passive techniques. They are "active" because they require that you start talking to strangers. You will open your mouth and speak. Scary, right? Well, not necessarily.

There are a few ways to make speaking to a stranger – finding the right words to use – easier. Definitely not foolproof, but easier. You can soften the "hardship" of talking to strangers using some of the simple techniques below.

1. Say "hi"

In my country, in my culture, it's uncommon to greet strangers. We just don't do that in Poland. When my father emigrated to Ireland, he was thrilled by the fact that complete strangers would see him and greet him on the street. The simple act of kindness was so amazing to him. It was a major reason he decided to stay there permanently.

If it's socially acceptable in your culture to greet a stranger, then go ahead and do it. Like the other techniques, aim for once a day to start.

2. Chip in

Another way to overcome your shyness is by joining an existing conversation. You don't have to think hard over your opening line. You don't have to seek an opportunity to talk or get their attention. The occasion and the topic of conversation are delivered to you on a silver platter.

Let's say you commute to work by bus, and hear two people complaining about the bus being late for a second time this week ... excellent opportunity to pitch in.

Perhaps you are in the cafeteria queue and you hear people discussing yesterday's football match. It just so happens that you watched it, too, and are a fan of the same team ... you have an in.

Maybe you are at the electronics store and you stumble upon two guys wondering if it's better to buy an Android or an iPhone. You use one of those – chip in and share your experience.

These are mundane, everyday situations in which you find yourself without any hassle on your part. You don't need to take much initiative. This can reduce your apprehension or anxiety.

3. A common denominator

Another way to ease the entry into conversation is to find that you have something in common with a stranger, something you can easily relate to. I already provided examples of the subjects I felt comfortable with; the people I felt a little less nervous about approaching. I hope you used my advice and recognized yours, too.

It's easier to start a conversation if you have several such topics prepared beforehand. You can even prepare a set of opening lines. For example, I have some about reading:

"Do you enjoy that book?"

"Have you read more books from this author?"

"Would you recommend reading that book?"

"I've noticed your book has an interesting title – what's it about?"

"What genres do you like most?"

Such opening lines start the natural flow of conversation. I love to talk about reading, so once I begin, I have no trouble continuing the conversation. There is no threat of an awkward silence in the middle of the conversation.

4. Compliment them

Everybody likes to receive a compliment. I've never met with rejection when offering praise to a stranger. No one has ever told me, "Get lost!" after hearing my compliment. The range of reactions is wide and mixed, but it's always in the positive spectrum.

So praise away. Look at the stranger and think, what could you praise. Their style, clothes or a cool tattoo? Maybe some behavior you admire?

Starting the conversation with a compliment may not be as rewarding as talking about the meaning of life, but it's an order of magnitude easier. At the beginning, your goal is just to open your mouth and speak to the stranger.

All those mental exercises you did previously will come in handy now. You contemplated the strangers in your mind long enough to have some ideas of what you admire in others.

I'm a healthy, straight, male – meaning, I notice women. When I see a woman in the morning and notice her beauty, I appreciate the fact that she likely woke up an hour earlier than me to create this perfect look. In the evening, when I feel half-dead, I appreciate a beautiful woman for her vitality. I appreciate small details they tend to apply to further enhance their look

– like fancy earrings or colorful patterns on their nails. Their imagination seems to have no limits in that regard. I appreciate this, because I lack it. The greatest effort I can muster to look good is to shave my face and iron my shirt.

I appreciate all parents, especially loving and patient parents with many kids. I know what it takes. I appreciate all the readers in the world. As they say, "All leaders are readers." You can clearly see that commuting every day on a train. Many people are taking naps, chatting, playing with their phones or staring idly through the windows. Then there is that handful of people reading.

I appreciate those who are kind, polite and who show their concern toward other people. Those who smile back at me warm my heart. I'm always eager to start a conversation with them.

Do you see what's happening here? There is not an ounce of shyness in the sentences above – very few thoughts of myself, my clumsiness or vices.

This attitude makes you want to speak to strangers. The grain of confidence Jim Rohn talks about, the confidence in others, is already present in you if you face life with this attitude. Others sense your confidence, your sincerity, and they answer with the same. The process of communication flows effortlessly, as it should between two beings who are created to seek and share love.

Sometimes, you may find people are confused or apprehensive, unsure about your motives, when you compliment them. Let's face it, we are not accustomed to random praise from strangers, it's an unusual situation. So, don't expect a great spiritual experience or for someone to fall into your arms when you compliment them. Usually, they will thank you and that will be the end of the conversation.

And that's fine. This book is a guide to overcoming shyness and gaining confidence, not a textbook on how to have a rewarding conversation each time you approach another person.

But, you will have rewarding conversations too. Since starting this journey, I've had a few conversations that touched me so deeply to leave me with tears in my eyes, conversations that still move me to this day.

5. Step it up again

There is a danger of convincing yourself that small-talk is OK. But, we are working here on overcoming shyness and developing confidence. Don't stop at the beginning of your self-improvement road. If you feel like talking about trivial things or giving random compliments is not enough, you are no longer being challenged. It's time to take it to the next level.

You want to become good at bonding, trusting and relationships, not at gossiping. Don't go into a frenzy about it. You don't need to go to a bad neighborhood and provoke some hoodlums to prove yourself, just take your daily discipline to the next level.

If all you are able to do so far is say "Hi" to one stranger a day, try to do it twice a day. Or, add a compliment to your "Hi." Something like:

"Hi, nice haircut."

"Hi, I like your shoes."

"Hi, you have slender legs." (Just kidding!)

Whatever you are doing now, do it more, do it better. If you are already comfortable with praising strangers, try to add a follow-up to each encounter. Compliment their outfit and ask where they got it. Praise their tattoo and ask how they got the idea for it. Compliment their child and ask something about their family life.

Or, create a challenge by approaching the people you feel most uncomfortable around. For example, I always had difficulty talking to attractive women, so sometimes I forced myself to approach one and start a conversation.

By the way, a funny story about this: my wife just asked me what I'm writing about now. I told her I am writing about talking to strangers, then added jokingly:

"I'll write about how to talk to chicks."

"But you are not talking to chicks, are you?" she asked, with a note of dangerous concern in her voice.

"OK, I will teach them to talk to chicks and not to tell their wives about it," I answered with feigned exasperation.

My wife literally growled at that answer. I said, "Oh, I should record that sound and put the link in my book to emphasize the point!" ;)

Anyway, to take it to the next level, you must try something new, something which makes you uncomfortable. That's the fastest way to grow.

Don't overdo it. Take it one step at a time. If you fail a few times in a row at the more difficult discipline, fall back to the old plan. The worst thing you can do is to decide that you "just can't do it," and give up. Consistency is the key. Do something every day, even if it's ridiculously easy for you.

Analysis – The Key to Success

You, **Under the Microscope**

Doing is enough, but analyzing your actions will boost your progress significantly. Therefore, analyze your progress, if not every attempt, then at least specific instances. Another successful strategy is to do an 'examination of conscience' at the end of each day.

When doing this self-examination, keep your subconscious at bay. Your brain loves apathy and you are trying to stimulate it to work, so it's only natural that it will rebel. Remember who you are — a shrinking violet trying to grow, not some lounge lizard. Fears of being audacious or brazen are unfounded. If you notice such signs, it's likely that this is sabotage perpetrated by your subconscious: "See how you shocked this poor man with your big smile? Don't do that anymore or people will think that you are a freak!"

Don't be afraid of being too bold. I assure you, it's a vain anxiety. I have practiced talking to strangers for over a year now and I still haven't banished all the old symptoms; boldness is still out of my reach. The only thing you should be afraid of is the fear; it's what stops you from trying. You are a shy person and you have communication issues. Look for the signs of them.

You should analyze your failures, keeping in mind this definition: Failure is not doing the thing you intended to do. The only failure is not trying.

Anything else is a success. Even doing something wrong is a success – it gives you valuable feedback. But, planning to say "hi" to two strangers and not doing so is a failure and you should contemplate what caused it.

You should expect some failures, especially when attempting any new technique. Every time you try to do something new, you are the most vulnerable. You are out of your league. Like a baby learning how to walk, it's highly probable that you will fall down some. So expect the failures, but don't anticipate them. Don't dwell on all the things that could go wrong. As I already mentioned, if something goes wrong, there's a valuable opportunity to learn within that experience.

Self-analysis is just the last step in the process, which looks like this:

1. A plan or goal

What are you going to do? Make eye contact? Smile? Say "hi?" Start a conversation? How many times? Once a day? Twice? As many as you can?

What do you consider a positive outcome of the practice? A stranger will keep eye contact for a few seconds? Will smile back at you or say something nice to you?

As I explained before, I have three different levels — smiling, chipping into an existing conversation, and talking with a complete stranger. I consider the discipline a success when at least one person notices my smile and reacts in some way – looks at me incredulously, averts her eyes or smiles back at me.

It's important to set such reasonable goals. Sure, I have managed to start conversations with a few strangers that delved into topics as deep as life and death, but it doesn't mean I have to do this every time. My life is full of chores, tasks and activities, and I assume yours is similar in that regard. You can't spend all your energy and willpower on a single discipline at the expense of your other obligations.

Other benefits of reasonable goals: teaching your brain consistency and vaccinating yourself against discouragement – our subconscious mind's favorite weapon. You probably know this internal dialog all too well:

"Oh, heck I forgot to do my 40 squats today!"

"Crap! You are such a failure; you can't even do 40 squats a day. Don't bother with doing them tomorrow. What's the use?"

Setting small goals allows you to meet them every day and disarm your subconscious.

2. Tracking system

You need a tracking system to succeed. Your chances dramatically decrease if you don't track your efforts. 'System' is a big word, but it can be as simple as a pen and a pocket notepad. Too low-tech? Then track your progress on your mobile phone using an app like Lift.do. Whatever works for you is fine – just stick with it.

It has to be quick and easy to use. If your goal is to smile at 30 strangers a day, then try using a tally counter app on your phone. Every time you push a specific button, the app's counter increases its value. That way you can keep the device in one hand, smile, and track your efforts simultaneously.

On the other hand, if you just want to converse with one person a day, it's enough to open your journal at the end of the day and jot down "done" or "not done."

I'm quite good at tracking, because I track a lot of activities in my life – 40 to 50 a day. What's more, I've tracked my "talk to a stranger" discipline for well over a year, so I'm accustomed to keeping my tracking system in my head until the evening, and then writing down the results. Practice makes you a master. I don't bother to litter my memory with the exact number of people who noticed my smile. I just mark the fact that someone did when it happens for the first time each day. But, I don't let that fact absolve me from my goal of seeking opportunities to talk to strangers later on (or to smile at them through the day).

While I don't keep an exact count of smiles, I do mark the exact number of strangers I talk to per day, because it's a low number. In fact, I don't recall having more than three conversations with strangers a day. It's low, so it's easy to remember.

Track. It doesn't matter if you are in the mood or not. If the tracking itself is too absorbing, simplify.

Don't complicate your life by introducing a complex tracking system. You should be able to record accomplishing your discipline as soon as it happens, and then come back to it when you have time for self-analysis.

3. Analyze

It's much easier to do self-analysis when you have data; that's what your tracking system is for. It is useless if you don't refer to it from time to time. You don't have to meditate or ruminate about your results every day, but it's not a bad idea. Consistency makes everything easier.

At a minimum, check every day if you've met your goal. As long as you have, you don't need to worry. Don't fix what's not broken. If you find yourself accomplishing your goals every day, it's time to think about taking the challenge up a level.

But, if you notice that you slacked off a few days in a row or regularly didn't meet your goals, that's the time for self-analysis. Again, don't listen to your subconscious too much. It wants to discourage you and get back to the "comfortable" *status quo*. It will happily use self-analysis for that purpose, if you let it.

Think rationally. Take a pen and paper, ask yourself questions, and write the answers down. Don't depend on your memory alone.

Some good questions for analysis:

What happened? Why?
How can I do it better next time?

Was it too hard? Why?

How can I make it easier next time?

What did I think before and after the "failed" attempt?

Did I forget? What kind of reminder could I use?

Was I simply indifferent to strangers? What do I need to increase my commitment?

Analyze your emotions and the facts surrounding your attempts and design a new way around the obstacles you stumbled upon. Track your results and analyze whether the changes help. Just don't give up. That's the ultimate failure.

I recommend dedicating a couple of minutes every day, in the same place and time, to develop your habit. Do your self-analysis sessions in writing. When you don't accomplish your goal, try to work out the reason and a solution.

It's important to not only focus on the debacles. When you achieve what you planned for the day, don't dismiss the positive experience. Reinforce it. Thank yourself, or thank God. Recall the experience in your memory, relive it. Write your success down in your journal and how it made you feel. Or find your own way to reflect on and reward your success.

The takeaway is to enforce the good results by focusing on the positives. This is the moment to let your emotions run wild. Celebrate your success!

The 21- Day Blueprint to Overcoming Shyness

My Plan or Yours?
I'm not a fan of 'success formulas.' I firmly believe, "to each his own." You have probably already noticed that the promises attached to most success formulas are ... well, just promises. What makes the formula successful is your implementation, not the formula itself.

My story and my experience will always differ, in ways large or small, from yours. You need to read, absorb and synthesize my content to come up with your most effective solution. Having said that, I know that a lot of people love ready-to-use recipes for improving their life. They may lack the energy or resolve to figure out their own unique way, but be willing to try an out-of-the-box solution.

I already had one such recipe completed before I began writing this book. I wrote it for Lift.do a number of months ago. I understand that not everybody enjoys jumping through various links while reading (myself included), so I made it a part of this book. However, if you want to give it a shot, I recommend joining Lift and joining this plan. The application is free, and the social accountability it provides really helps make a better you.

Not ready to build your own plan? Try my 21-day Success Blueprint:

The Blueprint: 21 Days to Success

Day 1: The reason

Everything starts with a reason. If it's good enough, it will make you take continuous action. It doesn't have to be set in stone; your reason may evolve as you evolve, but you have to have a starting place. There are as many reasons as there are people, but you need to find your very own. In autumn 2012, I started my personal development program and overcoming shyness was just one aspect of it. I started this discipline to develop myself to a higher level. My progress is very important to me, so that was enough for me to start.

So why do you want to overcome your shyness? Why do you want to talk to strangers? Does it have to do with your past? Do you want to change your future? Is it going to help you at work or in your relationships? Examine yourself. Find your own reason. Write it down. Easy does it; it shouldn't be longer than a single sentence.

Day 2: Notice other people

Start recognizing the people around you. Look at them and think about them. What things do you have in common? What things in them spark your interest? Write down a few of these.

Day 3: Observe other people

Stop being lonely in your own mind. Look at the people around and think about them. What do their actions say? How they are behaving toward you? If you had to compliment one specific man or woman, what would you say? Write this down.

Day 4: Eye contact

The first step in starting a conversation is to make eye contact. Stop avoiding other people's gaze. If you don't notice them, you won't talk to them. After successfully making and then breaking eye contact, give this person a minute of reflection. What things might you have in common? What things in them spark your interest? If you had to praise him/her, what would you say? Write these thoughts down.

Day 5: Your internal voice

You are a shy person, right? There is some internal resistance in you which prevents you from acting casually in the presence of strangers. You have to unearth your self-talk, your habitual thoughts when you try to talk to a stranger. So go and try to talk to someone. Just like that. Browse around, choose one person, quickly think of a line to start the conversation.

Start approaching the person. There can be only two outcomes: either you will start the conversation (congrats!), or you will talk yourself out of the idea. In that last case, I want you to listen carefully and remember what you are saying to yourself.

I was especially shy in approaching women. My thoughts were along the lines of: "What will she think of me? What if she freaks out: "Oh my god! Why are you talking to me, pervert?" Those are really irrational thoughts; your subconscious mind is not very brilliant. It's not the strength of these arguments which makes them effective, it's the negative feelings those thoughts trigger in your body.

If you have no experience in listening to your inner voice, I recommend a tool: Go to http://thefoundation.com/spi/ and provide your email. You will receive an mp3 on self analysis. You may first want to listen to the Smart Passive Income podcast, episode 85, to hear some background on the development of this tool: http://www.smartpassiveincome.com/how-to-finally-take-action/

Listen to the recording and repeat the exercise on yourself. Imagine approaching a stranger: be mindful of the unpleasant sensations in your body and interview your inner voice. Once you recognize what you are saying to yourself, it's much easier to deal with it.

P.S. Don't forget to continue making eye contact with strangers several times a day.

Day 6: Mental exercises

If you don't experience a breakthrough by analyzing your self-talk, you are probably still too shy to talk to strangers. That's fine, and perfectly normal. It took me several months to feel at ease talking to strangers (though I did not have the guidance that you have). Visualization can help you build this ease. Look at the people around you and think about them. Pick one person. Imagine approaching him or her and starting the conversation with some witty or engaging comment. Imagine that you are having a nice chat with the person. Finally, imagine that you are finishing your conversation and both of you feel at ease and enriched by the experience.

P.S. Don't forget to make eye contact with strangers several times a day. In fact, one of the people with whom you make eye contact may be part of your visualization. Reflect upon another person at least once a day.

Day 7: Philosophy

You read it right – philosophy. You need an underlying motive to continually approach new people and talk to them. To do this, you must be genuinely interested in people. You can't think only about yourself and be good in interactions with others. They pick up on your attitude. You can't be motivated by a desire to "learn how to manipulate people and then rule the world" (insert ominous laughter here), it just doesn't work that way.

I think a lot of my problems in talking to strangers came from my experiences being involved in Multi-Level Marketing as a teenager. I approached people, focused on selling my idea, and that totally didn't work.

Everyone is unique and, therefore, needs his own philosophy. Some people are extroverts; they have the curiosity of a child and ask questions all the time. I don't think any of these people need this particular plan, but their underlying philosophy might be curiosity: "I'm interested in people and their motives. That's why I talk to them."

My philosophy is the Christian philosophy – all people are my family. You need to find your own motivation. Your initial reason may not be enough to persevere in your commitment. Or maybe it will. Just ponder this from time to time, especially if you notice that you are slacking off in following this plan's guidelines.

P.S. Don't forget to make eye contact with a stranger several times a day. And practice visualization at least once a day.

Day 8: Smiling

The next important step in becoming sociable is using your smile. Often we are so locked in our fears and insecurities regarding other people that we don't notice they have their own struggles. We all are so isolated in our fast-paced society, and the simple act of smiling can knock down barriers. So, make eye contact and smile. You will be surprised by the mix of responses you will get. Whether the recipient of your smile recoils, looks away or smiles back, there is profound power in a simple smile.

P.S. Visualize your interactions once a day. Make eye contact with strangers. Smile.

Day 9: Practice

Visualize your interactions once a day. Make eye contact with strangers. Smile.

Day 10: Practice

Visualize your interactions once a day. Make eye contact with strangers. Smile.

Day 11: Practice

Visualize your interactions once a day. Make eye contact with strangers. Smile.

Day 12: Practice

Visualize your interactions once a day. Make eye contact with strangers. Smile.

Day 13: Practice

Visualize your interactions once a day. Make eye contact with strangers. Smile.

Day 14: Practice

Visualize your interactions once a day. Make eye contact with strangers. Smile.

Day 15: Practice

Visualize your interactions once a day. Make eye contact with strangers. Smile.

Day 16: Compliment

A compliment is an easy way to start an interaction. Pick one person today and give them a compliment. Anything, really. Perhaps their outfit, their hair, they way they make room on the bus for the elderly lady. The "what" isn't important, but keep it appropriate. Remember, too, starting a conversation with a compliment is rarely as rewarding as talking about the meaning of life, but it's an order of magnitude easier. Your goal is to open your mouth and speak to the stranger. That's the best start.

P.S. Visualize your interactions once a day. Make eye contact with strangers. Smile.

Day 17: Common denominator

Another easy way to open dialog is to find something in common with a stranger, something you can easily relate to. For example, I'm a reader and I LOVE to chat with other readers. I love to share reading experiences, to talk about books, authors, genres and styles. But I also spoke to strangers with smartphones when I was about to buy my first one. I'm comfortable with speaking to parents because, as a parent myself, I can relate to them. And so on. Think of the subjects you are passionate about, the topics which are easy and natural for you. Write them down; include them in your visualizations.

P.S. Visualize your interactions once a day. Make eye contact with strangers. Smile.

Day 18: Ask a stranger about himself or herself

It's a little more advanced, but still an effective strategy. People are eager to talk about themselves. Almost everyone is hungry for attention. People love to talk about their experience, share their opinions and talk about themselves. The good communicator may use it to his advantage. Start the conversation with a question about the stranger. One of my favorite lines is: "I've noticed you reading a book. Are you enjoying it?" And then I have a set of follow-up questions: "Why or why not? Do you recommend the book? Have you read more works of that author?"

Such opening questions are a great start and you can go even deeper after you start the conversation. I once began to chat with a lady sitting next to me on a train with my "standard opening." She was reading a book about disabled children. Then, I asked whether her job was related to the subject and, oh boy, what a rewarding conversation ensued! "Be prepared," as the Boy Scouts say, you may receive much more than you expected.

P.S. Visualize your interactions once a day. Make eye contact with strangers. Smile.

Day 19: Your first conversation

The exercises from the previous steps work, I assure you. But dry runs are good only up to a point. Today is that point. You can play it in your mind for hours, cooking up scenarios of conversations, but it won't substitute for the real experience. Today you must approach a stranger and start a conversation!

Well, if you're ready. If it really causes you great pain, practice your visualizations for one more week. And one more if you need it. Continue making eye contact and smiling. Every sustained action brings results. One day you WILL be ready to speak with a stranger. You don't have to do it exactly according to the plan; it must fit your needs. But ... the best way to overcome your fears is to face them. So why not face the challenge today? What is the worst that could happen by going through with it? Remember, the only failure is to not do what you set out to do.

P.S. Eye contact. Smiles. Visualizations.

Day 20: Did you fail yesterday?

No?! You really did it?! Congratulations! Keep up the good work! Continue your commitment. Talk to a stranger today and tomorrow; keep the momentum going.

What if you did fail? Well, it doesn't matter! Your past does not equal your future. You've gained valuable experience and you are one step closer to your goal. Take 10 minutes today, get a pen and a sheet of paper and analyze what happened. Did you panic? Why? What thoughts were running through your mind? you talk yourself out of trying? If necessary, go back step 5 and repeat the exercise I recommend there. Whether you have succeeded or not, don't neglect your tiny disciplines. Visualize your interactions once a day. Make eye contact with strangers. Smile.

Day 21: Rinse and repeat

You've reached the end of the plan, but your work is not done. Your goal wasn't just to talk to a stranger once in your life, was it? Rinse and repeat. Practice as long as necessary to make this habit automatic. For example, after a year of practice, I automatically seek to make eye contact with people around me. And whenever I look someone in the eyes, I smile. Talking to strangers shouldn't be something you need to achieve to prove yourself. It can be an activity which really adds value to your life and to the lives of the people you talk to. When you interact with others, miracles start happening!

Looking Forward

Following the above 21-day plan is not mandatory. I even claim that it should be your last resort. It may give you an idea of what progress in overcoming shyness should look like, but I'm 100 percent sure you can come up with a better plan for your individual needs and abilities. After all, it's your life.

If you are a shy person, you probably have some painful memories and experiences. These experiences are yours in an intimate way that I cannot comprehend. You need your own ideas and your own tempo to win your battles.

Whether you use my blueprint or develop your own action plan, the most important thing is to get the desired result: in time, you WILL be able to talk to strangers. But you won't achieve this result if you don't start, or if you start and give up. That's what The Ten-Minute Philosophy is for. Embrace it and you will progress.

Recommended additional lectures:

"The 7 Habits of the Highly Effective People" by Stephen R. Covey

"The Slight Edge" by Jeff Olson

A Toast to the New Confidant You

You need other people, you care about people, you are a part of society and you will not stop until you are sociable. Remember that you are your best cheerleader. You can't expect others to cheer you on, if you don't do it yourself.

Anchor this thought in your heart and mind:

As long as you try, success is inevitable.

The moment you stop trying, you've failed. But, remember that no reason is good enough to stop. Why resign if success is guaranteed? As long as you practice, you progress. Every day you try, you are closer to your goal. Sustained action always brings results. Don't defer it by giving your energy to doubts and hesitations.

When in doubt, keep a cool head. When moving forward, use your enthusiasm.

You will be unstoppable!

New Friends, New Blessings

The Gift of Giving

In February 2012, the millionaire Bernard Burchard launched a product, "Expert Academy." He put some free videos on the Web to promote the launch. Bernard gave a challenge in his video – he would give away five tickets to his event and pay for the winners' plane tickets. The challenge: make a video talking about five life lessons.

I decided to try. It would be the first video I'd ever made. I wrote the script while commuting on the train. One of the points to cover was: "Take action."

As I worked on the script, I noticed an old lady sitting next to me deep in prayer. I thought: "I pray every day, we have something in common. I will ask her about her prayers." At this point, my shy part reacted with panic: "Oh, no! That would be rude! It will be disaster! Don't do it!"

And I didn't.

After several minutes, I wrote the words "Take action!" in the script. This time I felt compelled to speak to the old lady. I did, and found out that she had two very ill grandchildren, one with heart problems; the other, autism. I learned that their parents struggle financially. I decided to take action, and I've been helping them financially since that time.

The old lady's son-in-law is an atheist; he more or less makes fun of her Christian beliefs. The fact that some stranger is donating money for his son, solely because the stranger saw his mother-in-law praying, is incomprehensible to him. It's totally contrary to his worldview, where everybody cares only for themselves.

He didn't convert to Christianity or anything, but this gesture is a breach in his philosophy. Maybe, with time, it will transform into something greater.

That year, I got Christmas wishes from them. The lady I talked to, the grandmother of those ill kids, prays for me every day. And I get tears in my eyes every time I think about it (even now, as I write this).

That was the first time my chat with a stranger affected my life and the lives of others, but it's not the last. That conversation happened when I really did not feel ready to talk to strangers. It was a great struggle. But rewards that blossomed from it – being able to help others, knowing that I am making a difference – were well worth the struggle.

Unnecessary Intimidation

As I mentioned, I'm especially shy around attractive women. On my commutes to work (when most of my opportunities for meeting strangers occur), I spotted a woman about my age, who frequently traveled on the same train. Every day, we would get off the same train and walk to the same bus stop.

Many times, I came up with things to say to her, such as complimenting her outfit, but I never had had the courage to start the conversation. I was too intimidated.

I was transferred to another office, and this office had a different entrance. This time, we got off the bus at the same stop and began walking the same direction. Thanks to this, I realized that we worked for the same company; we had more in common than just the same commuting route.

One Friday, she had a heavy suitcase with her. I assumed she was leaving for a weekend trip right after work. I wanted to help her out and start the conversation, but I talked myself out of it. You know, the standard stuff: "What will she think of me? She looks like a strong, independent woman – what if she is offended by my offer of help?" And hence, I missed that opportunity.

The train's timetable changed and I changed rail carriers. I saw her less often.

Several months after the occurrence (or rather non-occurrence) with the suitcase, I noticed her on her way from a bus stop to the train station. I was reading on the bus, immersed in my book, so I was a little surprised to see her.

I was now months into my talking-to-strangers practice. I was more confident. I started a conversation, using the most mundane opening line in the world:

"So, you work for the same company as me, don't you?"

We talked a little about work, about commuting and about the disreputable city district we walked by on our route from the train to the bus. We parted at the train station.

She was a normal, nice person, and the long months of apprehension were caused solely by my internal perception of myself and the flawed opinions I had about her in my mind. I never would have known, had I not found a common denominator.

True Depth

One day, traveling to work, I noticed that the lady sitting next to me was reading a book on an interesting subject – raising a disabled child. I started a conversation by asking about the book. She recommended it wholeheartedly. To keep the ball rolling, I asked her what her relationship was to disabled children.

She said she was a social or medical worker, I didn't dig for more details. Anyway, she worked with disabled children and their families on a daily basis. She told me how rewarding her job is. Some of her words: "pure love, simplicity, sincerity, no pretending, even ... mysticism."

I remarked how happy she seemed to have such a job. She confirmed this after a second of reflection. It seemed to be a kind of revelation to her. We talked a little more about the lives of disabled people, their families. We talked about life, and about God. It was a truly enriching experience.

Giving Inspiration

Another time on the train, a lady next to me was reading a paperback book in English. OK, a nice opening for me. I asked her how often she reads in English and where she gets the books. The conversation started to flow. Suddenly, she took charge, shooting a lot of questions my way: what do I do, do I have a blog, what is it about? It appeared that she was interested in personal development. She wrote down my blog address and name. I felt like I was giving my first interview.

I marked this conversation in my journal, because it was such a unique experience. That was on the 3rd of

December, 2013. We met again on the train a few weeks later. We talked longer this time; we live in the same town and talked the whole way to work. I had recently gotten the hard copy of *The Slight Edge*, with my story featured in it and I shared that with her. She again was full of questions. I answered them as best as I could. I told her my transformation story and explained to her the Slight Edge philosophy upon which I built my Ten-Minute Philosophy. She was inspired enough to buy her own copy of the book.

We are friends now and we meet on the train as often as our schedules allow, about once every couple of weeks. I shared with Kamila the success of "Master Your Time in 10 Minutes a Day." She was as shocked as I was by it.

Each time we talk, we discuss personal development, philosophy and our future ventures. A week ago, Kamila confessed that she had started a few daily disciplines inspired by my example and the Slight Edge philosophy. "I do 10 assisted push-ups every day," she said. "Until quite recently, I wasn't able to do a single one".

And how about that? An enriching friendship born out of a conversation with a stranger.

A Quick, But Meaningful, Moment

With time and practice, I became better at starting and carrying on conversations with strangers. I also became more confident. One day, I was on the train heading home from work. I hadn't talked to a stranger yet that day, so I was looking for the opportunity. I smiled at the lady sitting opposite me. She smiled back at me with a wide and sincere smile.

That's rare, at least in my country, on the 8 p.m. train, when everybody is going home after a long and (usually) tiring day at work. I estimate that only about one person in 20 smiles back at me on those evening trains.

"OK, level one checked off," I thought to myself. I stirred a reaction, so I accomplished the basic level of my discipline. I was done for the day. The train was approaching my town, so I got up, packed my laptop and put on my jacket. While doing this, another thought came: "What the heck? I should tell her that she has done something exceptional."

I sat down once again and said to her with a wide smile:

"Do you realize how special you are?"

She was abashed. I could almost read her mind: "WTF?"

She answered hesitantly, "No, why?"

"You smiled back at me. I smile at many people, but not many smile back at me. I think maybe one in 20. You are special."

"Well, thank you very much. It's what I do. I always smile back."

The anxiety left her. She was really touched by my remark. We had five minutes to talk about how people interact with each other. We had another common denominator – commuting – and we talked about that a little.

She thanked me a few times more for my remark. She said it made her day. It was a nice surprise for her at the end of the day. I started that conversation to appreciate her and I definitely succeeded. Two people felt better about themselves after this encounter.

Shared Interests

Another time, I noticed a lady reading *Ender's Game* on a train. She was determined. There was quite a crowd; she had to stand the whole way. But, that wasn't stopping her from reading. I immediately felt a surge of sympathy for her.

I was sitting half a car away, writing. I wasn't determined to talk to her at first. I saw her about 25 miles away from my town, registered the fact in my mind and went back to writing.

But this was an instance where preparation bears fruit. I had trained myself to notice people around me, so I noticed her. We both exited the train at my stop, the last station on the line. I caught up with her after getting off, and started the conversation:

"Hi, am I mistaken or did I see you reading *Ender's Game?*"

She nodded in assent. I asked her why she picked this title and the conversation started to flow. And, oh boy! It was the one of the best 'reading' conversations in my life. I accompanied her for a half mile or so, not exactly in the direction of my home.

We talked about our favorite books and authors, about genres we like and meaningful reading experiences. She was the soul mate of the reading part of my personality.

I utterly enjoyed that conversation; it was like talking with an old buddy. I hope to meet her again on the train and continue our conversation.

Confidence and Building a Business

Confidence is an amazing trait that helps you act with greater determination and focus. Like most authors, when I started writing, I fell victim to the impostor syndrome. I didn't feel worthy of teaching other people or sharing my experience.

Objectively speaking, I was a failure. I let complacency take over the better part of me. I was doing just enough to get by in my job, marriage, church and every other area of my life. I wasn't confident at all.

But, in life, everything affects everything else... The more I published, the more open I was, my results in talking to strangers improved. The better I was in talking to strangers, the better I got taking big, bold action in my writing ventures. I started my mailing list, joined several Facebook groups for indie authors, and began my official writer's blog.

Preparing my previous book launch, my marketing adviser recommended that I contact other bloggers and ask them for support. I felt extremely uneasy doing so, but I overcame my fears and reached out. People who knew me beforehand helped me without a moment of hesitation, but I was surprised to get some help from people who I didn't know at all. The book launch was an amazing success.

I discovered that getting to know people online is similar to getting to know them offline. While only a few of the bloggers I contacted were able to help me on the launch, I was enriched by every interaction with them.

I suffer from the impostor syndrome quite a lot: "I'm not a self-help guru. I didn't achieve much." The feedback trickling back from my readers is dismantling this attitude bit by bit, but I still experience trepidation when shouting my message out to the world.

While writing this book, I had my weekly Skype call with my accountability partner. It was the second week in a row that I failed to contact other bloggers asking them for help in promoting my Ten-Minute Philosophy. I confessed that it had more to do with my insecurities than with the actual lack of time. He said that this was an ideal case to show my readers this book. I hate when he is so right.

I mustered the courage and reached out again to my acquaintances. And again, I received support well beyond my expectations. They shared their success stories, some of them expressed interest in establishing a long term partnership, and some of them shared my idea with their followers. I overcame my anxiety and I touched the lives of people I would never have without this act of boldness.

Now go out into the world. Make your own success stories! I want to hear about them!

Jeanne

If you need a "first person" to talk to, you should try talking to the clerk that rings up your groceries or your fuel purchase. Usually people that hold these jobs are "talkers" like I am.

Liz

Realize that nobody really pays attention to you if you say something silly/off – it doesn't matter. Such realization is liberating.

If you stay away from the crowd, people think you are "stuck up" or conceited when they first meet you. If that idea horrifies you, that's cool – it's a great incentive to change.

Talk to chatty people. They are happy to have someone listen to them and they do most of the work. When you are finally comfortable (and perhaps bored), it is easier to make conversation with others.

Party survival tip: pick out someone at a party who looks more miserable/shy than you and cheer them up.

Peggy

I don't think so much about criticism from others, because I find 99 percent of people seem to either welcome the exchange or are indifferent and prefer to keep it short.

Free Gift for You

Thanks for reading all the way to the end. If you made it this far, you must have liked it!

I really appreciate having people all over the world take interest in the thoughts, ideas, research, and words that I share in my books. I appreciate it so much that I invite you to visit: www.michalzone.com, where you can register to receive all of my future releases absolutely free.

You won't receive any annoying emails or product offers or anything distasteful by being subscribed to my mailing list. This is purely an invite to receive my future book releases for free as a way of saying thanks to you for taking a sincere interest in my work.

Once again, that's www.michalzone.com

A Small Favor

I used to actively discourage my readers from giving me a review immediately after they read my book. I asked you for a review only once you began seeing results. This approach was against common sense and standard practice. Reviews are crucial for a book's visibility on Amazon. And my approach severely hindered me from getting my message out to people just like you, who stand to benefit from it.

I was convinced about that when "Master Your Time in 10 Minutes a Day" became a best-seller. Essentially, I've gotten a number of reviews in a short amount of time, but most of those reviews were the 'plastic' ones we all dislike on Amazon: "Great book! Great content! Great reading! Great entertainment!" Such reviews simply don't carry much weight; anybody could leave a review like that without even reading the book.

In the end, it didn't matter, and my book skyrocketed up the best-seller ranks, anyway. More people than ever have had the chance to get my book in their hands. I'm grateful for this, because more people have received the means to take control over their time and their destiny.

I want to ask a favor of you. If you have found value in this book, please take a moment and share your opinion with the world. Just let me know what you learned and how it affected you in a positive way. Your reviews help me to positively change the lives of others. Thank you!

About the Author

I'm Michal Stawicki and I live in Poland, Europe. I've been married for over 14 years and am the father of two boys and one girl. I work full time in the IT industry, and recently, I've become an author. My passions are transparency, integrity and progress.

In August 2012, I read a book called "The Slight Edge" by Jeff Olson. It took me a whole month to start implementing ideas from this book. That led me to reading numerous other books on personal development, some effective, some not so much. I took a look at myself and decided this was one person who could surely use some development.

In November of 2012, I created my personal mission statement; I consider it the real starting point of my progress. Over several months time, I applied several self-help concepts and started building inspiring results: I lost some weight, greatly increased my savings, built new skills and got rid of bad habits while developing better ones.

I'm very pragmatic, a "down to earth" person. I favor utilitarian, bottom-line results over pure artistry. Despite the ridiculous language, however, I found there is value in the "hokey-pokey visualization" stuff and I now see it as my mission to share what I have learned.

My books are not abstract. I avoid going mystical as much as possible. I don't believe that pure theory is what we need in order to change our lives; the Internet age has proven this quite clearly. What you will find in my books are:

— detailed techniques and methods describing how you can improve your skills and drive results in specific areas of your life
— real life examples
— personal stories

So, whether you are completely new to personal development or have been crazy about the Law of Attraction for years, if you are looking for concrete strategies, you will find them in my books. My writing shows that I am a relatable, ordinary guy and not some ivory tower guru.